From Behind the Stick

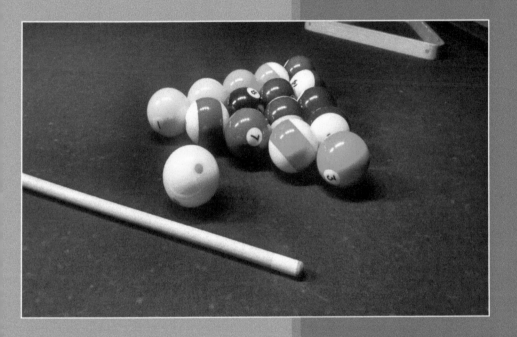

By

Marcos A. Carvajal

ISBN 978-1-64349-436-4 (paperback)
ISBN 978-1-64349-437-1 (digital)

Christian Faith Publishing, Inc.
832 Park Avenue
Meadville, PA 16335
www.christianfaithpublishing.com

Printed in the United States of America

To the memory of my grandfather and father

Carlos Jesus Carvajal
1914–2002

Carlos Jesus Carvajal Jr.
1943–2010

Rest in peace

Table of Contents

Chapter 1

The Question

It was almost dark when I heard my wife, Kristy, announced, "Marcos, dinner's ready!" That was all I needed to hear, so I put away the gardening tools. Pulling weeds seemed to keep my mind busy. It's something I do just as a stress reliever. I have been trying to grow a plush lawn for almost twenty years. Maybe I should plant some seed and fertilize? It was just a thought.

After a mildly busy day of yard work on a Labor Day weekend, I went inside, took a shower, made myself a nice tall glass of Cherry Pepsi, and had dinner. Just a little fatigued, I kicked back in my lounge chair to watch TV after eating. Nothing looked interesting, so I decided to play some pool with our youngest son, Zachary. It was a pleasure to play my most favorite game in the whole world with him. Zachary, being a ten-year-old, had been practicing and was eager to play. He is the youngest of our five children. Our oldest son, Kacey, had left to attend his second year of college but was still learning how to play pool himself. Although he was getting better, he still had lots to learn. He knew that because he had a really difficult time beating me. He could win every now and again but was not at all consistent. I enjoyed how he was so competitive during a match; it reminded me of my father.

Our oldest daughter, Elizabeth, the middle son, Joshua, and our youngest daughter, Victoria, had absolutely no interest in playing pool. Although I think they all would be really good, I didn't want to force them to play. I figured they would treat it like a chore instead of recreation. Kristy would play every once in a while, but she only had time for a game or two. She doesn't care much for the game, but when she has time, she will watch a few matches. She is actually a pretty good shot when she takes the time to play. Maybe she practices when no one is watching. Who knows?

Zach and I had been playing for about an hour or so when I received a text message from Kacey. He had informed me that a friend and he had entered a doubles pool tournament. The text made it seem that he was excited and nervous all at the same time. I have to admit I had the same feelings. I did know, however, because of his baseball background, he understood what kind of attitude you should have about winning and losing. After all, most games are set that way so kids can learn and get better. Zach shockingly asked me, "Is Kacey playing in a pool tournament?" I replied, "Yeah, hope he does okay," still feeling pretty nervous.

Then Zachary questioned me again, asking, "Dad, have you ever played in a pool tournament?" He took my breath away, but at that moment, I realized my kids didn't really know my story. It was this question that brought me all the way back to the year 1976.

Looking back, I never really thought about anything more than skateboarding, marbles, and basketball, much less pool; but I remember like it was yesterday, the first time I ever played the game of Carrom. I believe I was going into third grade when my sister and I attended a summer camp at our elementary school. We went because all of our friends from the neighborhood were going. Well, that's why I went. She probably went because my mom and dad said she had to. They had board games, card games, kickball, and dodge-ball. We could bring our bikes and skateboards on school property and actually ride them. These were different times, for sure. I think this summer camp was just set up to keep us kids from tearing up the neighborhood or keeping moms from killing their children, but that is just my adult opinion now. There's probably some truth to it, though. Needless to say, I had the best time. I always loved being outside and playing games—card games and chess to be specific.

Then, one day, one of the teachers took out this rather large piece of wood. It was huge, at least for a seven-year-old. It was about a two and a half square feet wood game board with net pockets in the corners. She turned it over, and there was a checkerboard pattern on one side and what looked like a kind of dartboard on the other. She began to explain the game to some of us kids that had gathered around her. "Set up the checkers on the board, just like you are going to play Checkers," she instructed. Then she gave us these two-foot sticks just a little thicker than a fountain pen and explained, "All you have to do is hit your checkers into the corner baskets on the opposite side of board before the other person."

I thought, *Piece of cake.* We began to play on this Carrom board, and I quickly noticed that no one else could do what I had thought to be a very simple task. Thinking really nothing of it, I began to play. The rules had stated that if you make a checker in the netted basket, you continue shooting until you miss. So I figured I will just make them all and not miss. I know it seemed so, pardon the expression, "elementary," but the game did not require much more thought than that. I had no problem with this game, and to be honest, I had a wonderful time beating everyone. I had not stopped to think that no one else was having any fun, but what seven-year-old notices that?

Toward the end of this weeklong camp, almost every game that was played had a sign-up competition. Everyone could pick any event or a game that they wished to compete in. You guessed it; I had entered myself for the Carrom board game. I can't remember if anyone was any good or if anyone gave me any real competition. All I remember is hitting every one of those silly checkers into the net basket. It may have been the first blue ribbon I ever won in my life. Well, maybe the first one I can remember. I'm almost fifty years old now, so the details can be a little fuzzy.

It wasn't long after that summer fun that my parents signed me up for the local Boy's Club, again, probably to keep me out of trouble. It may also be because my dad was extremely impatient with me. ADHD was not exactly a thing then, so my dad would fix any problems with vulgarity and the Navy's standard-issue belt that hung on the hallway door. Just thinking about it to this day still makes my stomach ache. I have described this to some of my adult friends, and one said to me that I may now have a form of PTSD. I don't know about all that, but it would explain why I have issues with my kids arguing or getting too loud in the house. Loud noises kind of set me off. Luckily, it doesn't happen that often. When my parents dropped me off at the Boy's Club, it was mostly because of basketball. I loved playing, and someday maybe I could become a Harlem Globetrotter. Not very likely, but no one ever said that I couldn't. So now as a five-foot-six Mexican from Yuma, Arizona, the chances of that dream coming true would be zero. While playing basketball at the club, I noticed they had two seven-foot pool tables. Most Billiard players call them "bar boxes," typically because they are commonly found in a bar, pub, or tavern. After every basketball game or practice, I would play pool while waiting for my folks to pick me up. This was just to pass the time. I never thought that I would take this game to any extreme level. After all, it was just another game. This continued, as I remember, for a few years.

During that time, the Boy's Club had a pool tournament open to just the kid members meaning no adults could play. Most of the boys that were members were under the age of fifteen. I think it was because typically at the age of sixteen most boys were getting a car or a job to buy a car. This was true in my case, but I digress. My dad let me play in the tournament, as he was unaware of all the playing I had accomplished in my idle time. He observed me playing pool every time we went to the bowling alley as a family, but not really paying any attention to how well I could shoot. So there might have been about eight or ten kids in this tournament. Not exactly a Vegas turnout, but for me, an eight-year-old, there might as well been a million other players there to beat me. It was my first time playing in a pool tournament. I remember being so nervous. Not being the tallest of eight-year-olds, the tournament director had allowed me to use the long wood benches to maneuver around the table. This did help me reach some fairly difficult shots that otherwise would not have been an option for me to shoot. I wish I could recall the play by play shots of every game that was played. All I can remember is the last kid I played was a teenager. He was more confident and much taller than I was. He probably thought, "There's no way this eight-year-old kid is going to beat me." I would have to admit I might have been thinking the same thing. My approach to Billiards was the same logic as the Carrom board game that I had been introduced to at the summer camp. Shoot all the balls in the pockets before the other guy does. Again, it seemed too simple. However, this approach apparently worked because I had won my very first tournament. The grand prize, as funny as it may seem, was a bottled Coke from the soda machine that was in the club director's office. I can promise you, winning the bragging rights of being a Billiard champion was worth the price of admission. Oh, I failed to mention, the tournament was free, and the Coke only cost a quarter, but that's not the point.

Chapter 2

The Addiction

Now Boy's Club was normally in the evenings. I'm not quite sure if it was all year, during school time, or in the summer. I had gained some interest in another game while I waited for my parents to pick me up. This game required some loose change, you know, nickels, dimes, or quarters. Some of us would stand in the street, about ten feet or so, away from the curb, turn toward the curb, draw an imaginary line, and pitch the coin selected to the curb. The closest coin to the curb wins! The other boys called the game "pitching." You could play with two or three people. I don't recall more players than that. The rules were simple, and the game was easy. I remember telling one of the other boys, "This is a lot like playing Marbles." I was an excellent Marble shooter. My dad had brought me some bank money sacks from his workplace when I was in second grade. He gave me these sacks so I could take my marbles to school and play with some of the other kids. In Marbles, when you win, you keep your opponent's marble. This pitching game was no different. When your coin was the closest to the curb, you would win all the coins. The best thing was when you got a "leaner," that means your coin is leaning against the curb on its side. If you're familiar with the game of Horseshoes, it's kind of similar. The odds of having two "leaners" at the same time were extremely rare, but when it happened, it would be considered a tie.

The game would definitely pass the time; however, I needed money to play. Having some money for me wasn't that uncommon. I scavenged the neighborhood almost weekly collecting cans and bottles for recycling money. I received nineteen cents a pound for aluminum at the recycling center. Having twenty dollars then was like having a hundred now. Sometimes, it blows my mind how hard and long I worked to collect some extra cash. After playing this pitching game for a few years, it became a huge habit. I also got really good at it. During recess at school, we would go in the restroom and pitch coins against the wall. Lots of kids lost their lunch money. Funny, now that I'm thinking of it, I can't remember seeing any sore losers run off and tell a teacher what was happening in the boys' restroom. Eventually, the habit became a part of me, and before I realized what was really happening, I had become addicted to gambling.

In 1979, the average school lunch was one dollar. My father would give my sister and me a five-dollar bill each to buy our lunch tickets every Monday morning. We could buy all five tickets for the week—one ticket per lunch with extra milk costing ten cents more. Instead of getting my lunch tickets, I would take my five dollars and run straight to the convenience store. Every Monday like clockwork, I would purchase five dollars' worth of Jolly Rancher Sticks. Those candy sticks were fifteen cents each. Most of the kids at school were not allowed to go to the convenience store, myself included. If my dad would have found out, I would have been dead meat for sure. During the course of the day, I would gradually solicit to anyone who was interested in purchasing some candy for a quarter. If you do the math, you'll find that my profit was around $2.50. This allowed me to eat and still gamble on a daily and weekly basis. Not bad for a ten-year-old, at least that's what I thought. Gambling had become more enticing the more I did it.

There were other games we could play when we didn't have much time. I learned to play odd or even, or, as some us kids called it, flipping. That's when two people flip coins in the air, and whoever calls it odd or even wins the coins. We did this mostly while waiting for the school bus to take us home. It became such a habit that I actually flipped silver dollars with a sixth-grade teacher at the bus stop in front of the school. Definitely, crazy times for me, it was all in good fun. Having an addictive personality was an unknown term to me; after all, I wasn't even going into junior high yet. What did I know?

Luckily for me around this time, the Atari 2600 was born; it was, by far, the best home video gaming machine of all time, at least for an eleven-year-old in the early '80s. Don't get me wrong. The real arcade games were awesome, but I was spending all my quarters on Donkey Kong, Galaga, and Defender. The only thing I had to show for it was the high score, until the store reset their machine. I asked my parents to get me this "most rad" system, and they both said, "Looks like you better save up some of your money, if you want it." I figured that would be the answer. My parents didn't go into debt to purchase luxury items, and to them, this was an unnecessary purchase. Now that video game cost around $150. I was doing the math. It took me over two months to have a twenty-dollar bill from recycling. So I figured I would be married before I could ever buy it. After giving it some thought, I could mow lawns or maybe get a paper route. My goal was crystal clear—get an Atari or die! My dad knew how badly I wanted it. He agreed to let me purchase it if I bought it with my own money.

Dad invited the distribution manager that employed kids to deliver local newspapers into our home. I was still too young, but my dad told him I would be having a birthday that month. They both agreed that I could take on this new responsibility. "This is great!" I proclaimed with pride. So I ended up with a paper route and worked daily toward my goal. My paper route would allow me to make sixty to seventy dollars a month. It would only take an hour or two a day. Now that I'm thinking about it, that is only one dollar an hour. Crazy stuff, huh?

Still collecting recyclables and mowing the neighbor's yards when I found the time, I continued to make extra money. What I thought would take decades I had accomplished in a period of three months. I remember how proud I was when my dad took me into the Thrifty drugstore to buy the Atari 2600 video gaming system and a small black-and-white TV. My focus had taught me patience and diligence. My dad seemed a little upset, probably because I just spent two hundred dollars on what most parents would consider to be a waste of money. If you think in today's dollars, it was like spending one thousand dollars. But I was twelve; I never thought it was a waste of money.

I kept that paper route for the next five years. The persistent work ethic, which my parents had instilled in me, paid some high dividends. That job helped me buy games for the Atari system, music, clothes, and my first car. Staying focused is a good thing, if it's on something productive. My mom had explained to me how to make smart purchasing decisions once I started making some money. She said, "Ask yourself three questions: Do you need it? Can you afford it? Can you pay cash?" She also told me that I should wait at least a week before buying anything that was a big purchase. This was to prevent any spontaneous purchases. I had no idea that, in all that time, I was developing character.

Most of my friends lacked the discipline required to achieve anything. I didn't blame them. It wasn't exactly their fault. There is one thing that I had that they did not—my father. My dad didn't believe in raising a lazy kid. If I did not do what I was supposed to do or what I said I would do, it was the belt or some other form of discipline. I knew, for a fact, that I did not want that! I forgot to mention, I still have my Atari 2600 and *all* the games after all these years. My kids still can't beat me at Kaboom; it's our favorite, along with Circus Atari. The boys love to watch the . . . *Splat!* when your player dies. Now that's fun stuff. Besides, I don't even know how to hold the gaming controllers for a Playstation or Xbox.

Chapter 3

The Old Man

Playing games seemed to be a part of my DNA. My dad loved all types of games. My sister and I were raised on playing board games, like Clue, Life, Aggravation, and Pay Day. My sister was always more partial to brain games such as Jeopardy, Trivial Pursuit, and, my dad's favorite, Scrabble. As a family, we played lots of card games—Spades, Hearts, Pit, Uno, Rook . . . just to name a few. It is fair to say that my gaming muscle was really in shape. When I was younger, I can recall playing Dominos with my sister and dad. I didn't understand the game the same way they did. I just matched the numbers to the open location when I could. After a while of playing, my dad would make announcements of which domino I was going to play, as if he could see what was in my hand. Being a little frustrated, I asked him, "How do you know what I'm going to play?" He said, "All you have to do is count. It's the process of elimination." Then he specifically mentioned, "You have to really pay attention to what has been played and when someone passes." He was talking about strategy and anticipation of the opponents moves. As a kid, you can't possibly understand this. Or can you? I started learning and understanding the game more and more. It wasn't long that my sister and I were actually beating him. Not just at Dominos but all games. He would get mad when he lost, kind of like a little kid, but my sister and I did not care. That was our primary goal, to beat Dad; and, of course, like any kid, we would relish in our victory. Don't get me wrong, we didn't win very often, but when we did . . . it was an epic scene.

Growing up in Yuma has advantages—you never have to wonder if it will rain; it won't. Most often, we just had to consider if the monsoon winds and dust storms would take part in any outdoor activities, like golfing, hunting, or froggin'. Yup, I said froggin'. It's actually called "frog gigging," but no one says it that way. In October, Dad would take my sister and me out around midnight to go froggin'. Dad would get his high-powered flashlight, plug it into the truck cigarette lighter for power, drive slowly on one side of the canal, and point the beam of light on the opposite side of the canal bank. While he was doing this, my sister and I would walk down the side of the canal Dad was shining his light on. If he shined a light on a frog, the light would paralyze the frog briefly. That was just long enough for someone, like myself, to sneak up behind it and stick a twenty-foot gig in its back. Once the frog was on the gig, I would pull it off the barbs and put it in the knapsack my sister was carrying. We would get about twenty frogs. It's still some of the best meat I've ever had—looks like fried chicken, has the texture of shark, and taste like lobster. If you have not tried it, you are definitely missing out.

Yes, the heat played a part, but when you're from one of the hottest cities on the planet, you get used to it. My dad had given up softball and began playing golf when I was eight years old. He would take my sister and me to the local driving range at night so he could practice. I would watch him hit balls for hours. Then we would all go to the putting green to work on our short game. I say "we," because my dad would let me putt with him. Since my dad had given up softball and started playing golf, weekends were kind of dedicated to going golfing, instead of taking the family to church. Of course, he would take a break from golfing when hunting season started.

So we, as a family, didn't go to church as often as we had in our earlier years. We would go intermittently and always on the normal occasions, such as Easter and Christmas. Although we all believed in Jesus, he wasn't exactly a priority. I am glad my parents understood that they needed the family to have a moral compass. Dad was not exactly a spiritual leader. He would say before we answer to God, we have to answer to him. His favorite verse was Proverbs 13:24, "Whoever spares the rod hates their children, but the one who loves their children is careful to discipline them." He was *not* afraid to discipline, I can promise you that. His idea of teaching us the Bible was watching movies like *The Ten Commandments* and *The Greatest Story Ever Told*. My favorite is *Jesus Christ Superstar*. Dad wasn't a fan, because it's a musical. Mom and Dad may have taken their own road instead of following God's will, in some cases, but as an adult now, I have caught myself trying to do things my way too. I have also noticed it normally does not work out too well. To this day, I am glad to say my sister and I believe that Jesus is our Lord and Savior. So, I guess, Dad didn't do such a bad job raising up the next generation.

By the time I was in high school, I had been golfing with my father for five years. My normal day on the course was an 80 or 84. It was nothing extraordinary, but not too shabby for a teenager. I ended up playing on the varsity team for four years and graduated as a letterman. Golfing and hunting was about the only things my dad and I could do without being annoyed with each other. All the days and hours we spent on a golf course or got up early to go dove or quail hunting were priceless. He cherished every moment, as did I. Dad seemed to beat me at golf a majority of the time—even in his later years before he died.

My dad was born in November of 1943, in Yuma. He saw the town grow so much. He would complain about it constantly. His dad, my Tata, worked hard at the railroad for many years raising five kids of his own. My dad was the oldest son of the crew. Back in those days, he would say, "If you don't work, you don't eat." He was always talking about how he started picking cotton at the age of seven. I am sure that was the case. It seems my dad was one of the hardest-working men I knew. Although, Uncle Al, my dad's brother, is a pretty close second. I asked my dad, "How come you can't play pool?" He was a bit upset with me after I had asked. Not knowing, I may have struck a chord about his upbringing. He explained to me that when he was younger, Tata would hustle pool to make extra money to feed and clothe the family. Tata played travelers and vagabonds that were in transit by the railway station. He further explained that playing pool in those days was not the environment you wanted your children around. So, consequently, his dad wouldn't let him play. Tata would have beaten him silly if he was caught anywhere near a pool hall, card table, or bad people like that. He told me, "You have it good. There are pool tables in every bowling alley and family fun centers everywhere you go." He continued, "Back in my day, there was no such thing as a family fun center." Don't get me wrong, my dad could play pool just as well as the average person, but he wouldn't be considered a threat if he was in any competition.

Out of this conversation, all I heard was, "Tata was a pool hustler?" Remember, at this time, my parents still did not know about my gambling habit. So this information intrigued me. How come no one mentioned this before? I asked my dad, "Do you think Tata could teach me?" He was hesitant in his response. He thought for sure there was no way Tata was going to teach his grandson what he did not teach his own son. "Can I ask him when we go over to Nana and Tata's house?" using my adolescent begging voice. All my dad said was, "Don't count on it!" I could not wait to ask but was a little hesitant because of what my dad said. Tata could be stubborn and difficult to deal with, too, just like my dad. But I just had to know.

Chapter 4

The Mentor

We went over as a family to Nana and Tata's house to visit or eat. It was a fairly common occurrence. We would normally sit around the TV as my mom and dad talked. They were usually watching boxing or a soap opera, but the shows were always in Spanish. They spoke Spanish most of the time, especially when they were talking about my sister and me. They would address us occasionally, and then they would speak English so we could understand. Looking back at these visits, as an adult, I wish I had the foresight to ask more questions. But, at that time, the only question I had on my mind was for my Tata.

He loved telling jokes. It was always fun listening to him try to tell us a joke. I say, "Try," because he would always tell it in Spanglish, and he would burst into uncontrollable laughter before he could get to the punch line. I wonder what the jokes were about. It really didn't matter; we would all laugh just because he was laughing so hard. It looked like he was going to pee his pants. It was quite entertaining. Sometimes, I still hear that giggle of his, and I just have to smile.

Now I was around eleven when, for some reason, my family and I went to watch a baseball or softball game in Tucson, Arizona, right off I-10 and West Ina Road exit at some sports complex or something. I really was not interested in watching the ball game. That is probably why I don't remember why we went, but I remember there was a small seven-foot coin-operated pool table in the clubhouse. Once I saw that, I could have been there all day. Nothing else at that time mattered. I do not remember how many games or how long I played, but what I do remember is that it was fifty cents to play a game. There was this other kid who wanted to play against me. I think he was just a little older than myself, maybe thirteen or fourteen. So we had decided to each put a quarter in to have a game. We flipped for the break, of course, and I won the break. The reason I remember this game is it was the very first "break and run" that I had ever had. Needless to say, the other kid was not very happy, but I did not care. I ran down to the bleachers to find my parents. I needed to tell them what I had done; I could barely breathe, because of how excited I was. You would think, just the sheer excitement that I had would bring a parent joy to hear that their kid succeeded at something, but that would not be the case in this story. Nope. All I received was, "That's good. Go back and play."

Apparently, it was all I could talk about on my way home. Somehow, my Tata had heard about it. Before I could ask if he could teach me to play, he came up to me and said, "Would you like me to show you how to play real pool, not this 'Bar Banger' stuff that you do with your friends?" I didn't understand what he was referring to, but it was okay. I didn't know much of anything at eleven years old, anyway. He handed me a book called *Winning at Pocket Billiards*, by Willie Mosconi. I can't even tell you how many times I have read this book. It had pictures too! Tata would invite me to go play at a few different places. One was called Lutes Casino, and the other was The Golden Cue. Both had tables that were huge and in pretty rough shape. We would play once or twice a month for an hour or so. Almost the entire time we had a table, he would show me shots that I needed to learn and practice. Tata had been retired for some time by the time he started teaching me how to really play pool. He had lots of physical ailments; the big one was his in his right arm. He told me that the ball and socket joint was deteriorated from playing so much pool. At least that's what he told me. It could have just been a reason why he missed a lot of shots, but I do not think that was the case. He wouldn't stop taking the shot he was trying to teach me until it was executed correctly. Once he demonstrated the shot, then he would expect me to duplicate it. Sometimes, I could execute it quickly. Other times, not so much. His body would only allow him to shoot for an hour or two. I could see that he wished he could keep on playing, but I always noticed him grimacing after a while.

By the time I was in high school, I could run a rack about 30–40 percent of the time. Around my sophomore year of high school, I had a friend on the golf team that said his dad was selling their pool table. They only wanted seventy-five dollars for it. I told my dad I could buy it, if he allowed me to. He agreed and helped pick it up and put it in the back of the truck. We had a perfect spot on our backyard porch to place it. I was so happy; I could play whenever I wanted. Who cares if the table was outside? Oh? Apparently, Dad did. My dad was so awesome; he built a room around the table so we all could play inside. Now, when my Tata came over, he would set up shots and show me how to execute them, and when I say execute, I don't mean make the shot. I mean, I make the shot and get the proper leave or position for the next shot. I don't know how many times he would walk in, look at me, and ask, "Are you ready?" This meant get your cue stick. He would set up a shot, pull a dime out from his pocket, and flip it onto the table. Once the dime had stopped, he would put a chalk mark where the dime was and proceed to tell me, "Now stop the cue ball there!" Again, sometimes it would take me minutes and sometimes hours.

When he left the house, if I had completed the task or not, I always saw a proud look in his eye. I figure that could have been the driving force that kept me behind the stick for all those early years. Funny, no matter how good I thought I was getting or even how good I was, he always seemed to kick my butt. To this day, I don't know how that was possible. I can hear that unmistakable laugh right now as I am writing this. He had such a passion for the game. If he left me anything, it's a love and passion for the game of Billiards. I hope and pray I can pass this on to my future generations, God willing.

Chapter 5

The Lessons

Having a table of my own to practice multiple shots and getting out of difficult leaves was extremely beneficial. My best friend, Allan, would come over to shoot some and hang out. When we had parties, people would want to enjoy a game or two. The best thing was learning the art of playing great pool. I would spend hours on a "bank shot" or a "rail shot" just so I could watch the action on the cue ball. When we installed the pool table, my Tata came over with a special cue ball for me to practice with. He gave me strict instructions to *not* use this specific ball to break with. He further explained that the ball was a little lighter and smaller than a normal cue ball. He had me take a shot so I could feel the difference. Right off the bat, I realized that I would need to learn how to control my stroke and ball speed. The action on this special cue ball was exaggerated. Meaning, that if I applied bottom English to draw the ball back, it would come back farther and faster than what a normal cue would do. If I stroked the ball with left or right English, the ball would take an enhanced deflection in a way that was unexpected. It's hard to describe. Let's just say that I could make the ball do more because my novice cue stroke was not developed enough to control a normal cue ball.

Tata told me that the key to playing great pool was controlling the cue ball, and with this ball, it would help me gain knowledge of what cue English can do when applied correctly. He gave me instructions on how to develop a straight stroke and how to build up an understanding of ball speed. The drills are elementary in nature but exceedingly difficult to execute. The drills would frustrate me as I practiced. I would become more and more determined to accomplish and perfect what I had chalked up to be an easy endeavor. Nothing was further from the truth. These drills that I am going to outline and illustrate have a purpose. That purpose and reason is consistency, control, and most of all patience. While Tata and I played, he would always say, "Don't be in a hurry to lose!" It didn't make sense to me either; I will explain this in the next chapter.

I'm not going to talk about how to hold the stick or where to stand or how you keep everything balanced before you shoot. Don't misunderstand me. All those things are important, but what I'm going to address is the simple fact that most players "think" they hit the ball straight when they supposedly hit the ball—"straight." This is not explained anywhere much. So I am going to try to shed some light on what it is that I am talking about. Most players don't practice shooting the ball straight. My Tata had told me that if I were going to have any consistency, I would need to learn how to stroke the cue ball so there would be no transferred English. Let me explain further. When shooting what appears to be a perfectly straight shot, you're unaware of the transferred English; when shooting, the cue ball is typically spinning in a specific direction. The spin direction is not important at this time; just know that most people apply spinning from the cue stick to the cue ball. As soon as the object ball is struck by the cue ball, the spin of the cue ball is transferred to the object ball. What I have just explained is actually called "physics." Unfortunately, the average player really thinks the game is only geometry. Tata had explained to me that Billiards is 10 percent geometry and 90 percent physics. This would explain why so many people who try to play pool are not very good.

The stroke drill helped me to make the adjustments I needed to keep, not only the cue ball from spinning offline but also how to keep my cue stick level and through the ball. The result—my stroke stayed consistent. When doing this drill, I was told to practice striking the cue ball with different speeds. I will illustrate so you get the idea. I needed to be patient and continually focus on where I struck the cue ball. I continually tried to strike the cue ball in the center. It sounds easy, right? I found it to be an extremely difficult task.

The stroke drill is designed to help keep a "straight shot" straight. In the top table illustration, the cue ball is right on the head spot. I would then grab any two object balls from the rack and place them about two or three ball lengths next to the cue ball on the left and the right. These two balls are in this drill to act like a goalpost.

I would then hit the ball to the center of the footrail, marked with a blue dot. The object is that the cue ball hits the footrail and comes between the goalpost balls, hitting the head-rail in the center, also marked with a blue dot.

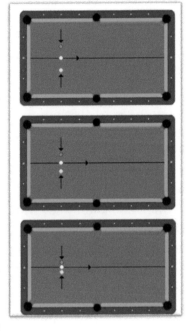

In the middle table illustration, the goalpost object balls have been moved closer together. This is by design. My objective is to make it between the goalpost every single time I stroked the ball. If I could do it a minimum of ten times in a row, I would be on my way to establishing a perfectly consistent stroke.

The bottom table illustration is the ultimate challenge. I placed the goalpost balls a half-inch away from the cue ball and make it through without hitting the balls. If I could accomplish that ten times in a row, I would have obtained a perfect stroke. This takes lots of time, so I would remember not to rush. I was amazed with the results, not only with the drill but also when I applied it to my game.

By doing this drill, my muscle memory was taking over during game play. This resulted in making longer, straighter, and more consistent shots. Every pool player knows the hardest shots are the long straight ones. Tata would say, "Looks easy, doesn't it? Good luck!"

I had mentioned in the last chapter how my Tata would come in the house, put his hand in his pocket, pull a dime out, and flip it onto the pool table. He then would set up the same shot every single time and instruct me to leave the cue ball on that spot after making the shot. He left the dime on the table while he was there. He would patiently watch me as I continually tried to execute the shot challenge that was before me. If he had to go, he would mark the spot with chalk and take his dime with him. I was told to leave the cue ball within a dime length of the spot. That's crazy stuff, right? Before Tata was able to do that at my house, he would set up this "ball speed" drill at the pool hall. We would do this drill before we actually played. He taught me this before I was in high school. This drill had to be the most intense drill I have ever done to this day.

Let me explain the drill; then I will illustrate. He would set an object ball close to a corner pocket but not too close. He would set it just close enough that I was more focused on the leave and speed of the shot than I was on making the shot. He would put the cue ball at an angle in such a way that the shot was never straight in. The cue ball would be close to the center of the table and a foot from the headrail. It didn't have to be on the center. It really didn't matter. The cue ball was always about two to three feet away from the contact point of the object ball. Once the shot was set up, he would start by dissecting the table into halves. Then he would put the tip of his stick in the part of the table he'd want the ball to stop in after I made the shot. After I executed the shot ten times, he would then put the tip of his stick into the remaining section, instructing me to shoot ten more in the target area. Here is where it gets interesting. He would ask if I was ready and warmed up. I would say yes, because I already knew that he was about to draw a fictitious line through the middle of the table. Now the table was in four sections, so he would have me continue to make the same shot over and over but have the cue ball stop in a different quadrant. I did this drill literally, for years. I'll show in the illustration how fine-tuned I had to be to have perfect ball speed and get the leave that I planned on. I still love it when I hear someone say, "Lucky leave!" They have no idea how much work that took.

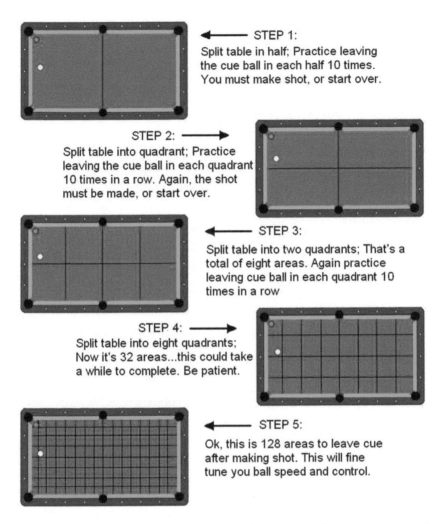

STEP 1:
Split table in half; Practice leaving the cue ball in each half 10 times. You must make shot, or start over.

STEP 2:
Split table into quadrant; Practice leaving the cue ball in each quadrant 10 times in a row. Again, the shot must be made, or start over.

STEP 3:
Split table into two quadrants; That's a total of eight areas. Again practice leaving cue ball in each quadrant 10 times in a row

STEP 4:
Split table into eight quadrants; Now it's 32 areas...this could take a while to complete. Be patient.

STEP 5:
Ok, this is 128 areas to leave cue after making shot. This will fine tune you ball speed and control.

So getting the leave after any and every shot becomes more of a learned response to an arduous and repetitive drill. When I tell people how many hours I did this drill as a kid, they can't believe it. When I got older, I would change the initial setup shot that I've shown in the illustration, but I would continue to practice leaving the cue ball in a specific spot.

Since I had the ability to spend hours on end taking the same shot over and over again, I also learned what happens when I missed. This is an art in itself. When I missed certain shots the object ball actually went into other pockets that I had not considered. If I did this shot enough times, I found that it becomes a real shot in a game. Most opponents wouldn't even consider that the object ball would go into the pocket I told them I was shooting at, much less have it really go in. This is what my Tata called "the art of the miss." This becomes a real handy tool when I was in the process of hustling an opponent. It's a wonderful way to make a win look like an accident.

Because I had learned how to shoot so well, the downside was that no one ever wanted to play pool with me. My dad would shoot a few games with me, but not for long periods of time. Allan would shoot for long periods of time, but mostly because he had nothing better to do. After a while, he didn't really want to play either. My sister would play, and she would get to be a decent player, but I don't know if she ever has had a break and run. She said they used to call her "Side Pocket Annie" when she played in college. She found out few people knew how to actually play. Lots of people shoot pool, but few know how to play pool. I tell friends all the time, "Just because you know how the Chess pieces move, doesn't mean you know how to play Chess." There is a strategy involved that most are unaware of. Just like when I used to play Dominos with my dad. Once he explained to me the concept of strategy, not just putting the pieces in their proper place. All of the sudden, I could not only score, but I could win.

I had become hungry to play all the time. It seemed that I was always looking for any excuse to play someone. Even to this day, I struggle to find someone who wants to play. Everyone always says the same thing when I ask them over to shoot a few games. "I'm not very good," as if I thought they were professionals in a past life. I just love playing. Seems to me, my kids may be the only ones who will play with me. Hopefully, they'll want to learn the whole game, not just shooting.

Chapter 6

The Hustle

After learning how to play pool and fine-tuning my control of every shot, the game seemed to be a thousand times easier than the "just-make-all-your-balls-in-before-the-other-guy" mentality. Remember, I had already been playing games for money. Most of the money I had was earned from my paper route, recycling, or mowing lawns on my own. My parents didn't know I was playing pool for money. Not a lot of money. It would start around a dollar a game and maybe get to five dollars a game. That was extreme for a kid in the early '80s. I'd win some and lose some. That's why it's called gambling. I would really try to win all the time. I did my best in those early years. I was probably between the ages of eleven and thirteen. At the time, my Tata was still teaching me the drills I explained in the previous chapter. I continued to play people for money, not so much for the love of the game of Billiards, but more so for the love of the money. It gave me an adrenaline rush. Finding someone to play, having one game or agreeing on playing a set for a specific amount of money, was a new challenge. I had not prepared myself for really playing for money, although I could shoot well enough to keep up with most players. I was still lacking a skill that would allow me to win consistently. That skill has a name. It's called "hustling."

Pool hustling is a completely different game than Billiards. Some would think that they are the same, but I would have to disagree. Let me explain. When I play a game of pool now, it is for sport and entertainment, not for any personal gain other than enjoyment. Enjoying a game of pool will not typically make your opponent feel badly about themselves. Nor is there any form of deception or manipulation going on that would almost guarantee that I would walk away the winner. Pool hustling is not the same as gambling. When I was gambling, the odds were typically equal or not in my favor at all. When I was hustling someone, I was almost certain to leave triumphantly. I recall an earlier time when my dad let me watch a movie called *The Hustler*. It was a fascinating movie about two pool players who wanted to be the best shooter around, and they would play hours on end to prove that they were the best. Yes, they played for money, but there was an aspect of the movie that I had misunderstood. In the movie, the two players knew each other could play well. There was not any deception about the level of their ability. This kept the game intense, but there was still a level of respect for each other. This is when you hear terms like "It's a gentleman's game." I heard it more on a golf course, but it carries the same meaning and understanding in a pool hall. As an immature kid watching this movie, I figured I could play pool to make more money. I just needed to get better at shooting so I wouldn't lose. When I walked away from a pool table, I wanted everyone to know I was a better player than they were. So I became a little cocky and arrogant, to say the least. My ability to play was fine, but something was missing. I was still gambling. I had not learned to hustle pool.

At some point, my Tata had taught me what I'm about to share. One of the first things he said was, "Don't be in a hurry to lose." I mentioned this in a previous chapter. He was talking about setting up shots instead of trying to run the balls all the time. He would say, "Why would you run four, five, six, or seven balls, and then miss to only leave an open table for your opponent." He continued, "If you can't run them all, then don't run any. Set them up and wait for your run out." He compared it to an overanxious Chess player who moves their queen in position to place the other player in "check" just to have that player take their queen with a pawn. He asked, "That's not productive, is it?" What he was talking about was being more patient instead of trying to force a fast game or a run. This was the huge piece that I was missing. Of course, that was just the beginning.

Remember, hustling has a level of deception. As a parent, we call it lying. There is a recipe for pool hustling, as I will explain. It's as if it were in a step-by-step cookbook. I know the recipe, and just like most things I cook up by following the recipe, it comes out the same almost every time. I learned these steps sometime before high school. My dad knew that Tata had taught me how to hustle people while playing pool after I joined the military. My dad wasn't too happy about it, and he expressed some thoughts toward me about it, but I will talk about that a little later.

There were some prerequisites before I was able to pull off a successful hustle. I must know how to shoot and control the cue ball as I explained in chapter 5. If I could not play well, none of these steps were going to help me. I needed to have some money that I was willing to lose. Let me explain. Most people in the pool hall are what a hustler would call a "fish." Meaning, everyone is and can be a potential prospect to be hustled; but to reel in a fish, I needed some bait. There's work involved with fishing that needs to be done in order to obtain some bait. I would need to dig up worms or spend money on a lure in order to attract the fish. It's no different in a pool hall. The bait is the money, and having extra money to lose will dictate how much money I could potentially walk away with. My Tata showed me not just how much to have but where to put it. Again, these are the things I needed to do even before I got to the pool hall. He told me if I was planning on winning big, I would have to mentally prepare. He told me that when I put money in my pocket, to put all the smaller bills under a twenty-dollar bill. I will explain why in the steps. He continued to tell me to carry extra cash, but to have it in a different location on my person, like in my shoe or under my hat. He explained that I had to be willing to lose and to not run the tables. This wasn't what I was doing before. Remember I was trying my best to beat my opponent by running out the table or just playing pool better than my opponent. He instructed me to make sure I never take my own stick to play. This bummed me out because I liked playing with my own stick. He would further tell me that once inside the pool hall, to play on a table that was close to an exit but away from other tables. He explained that some people may retaliate by using physical force, and I may need to leave in a hurry. He said to play away from other tables so I wouldn't scare the rest of the fish away. And, finally, he told me that whatever I do, to never ever make it look like I know what I'm doing. Out of all the things he said, I knew this last thing was, by far, going to be the most challenging, especially for this egotistical, arrogant male teenager. I'm sure I could find some family and friends who would vouch for my character, or should I say lack of?

So off to the pool hall I go. I'm supposed to look like I am clueless, right? I need to make sure I look and act like all the other fish. No one needs to know that I'm actually a fisherman. To pull this off, I had to understand it's just an acting job, and like most actors, I wanted to be paid for my performance. Now I walk into the pool hall and look around the room as if I was disoriented. I didn't go to the counter and get a rack just yet. I made it appear that I'd never been there before. While standing still in the entryway, I would gaze aimlessly around the room. Taking notice of how many fish were there and where the fish were located in the room. If I did this long enough, someone who was working behind the counter would ask me if I wanted a rack. If not, I would go to the counter and ask how much it costs to play. Most players that shoot don't care how much it costs. Only beginners and non-pool players typically ask for the rates. Once I had a rack of balls, I would turn and look at the tables again. I had picked out the table I wanted after I walked in and gazed aimlessly around the room. I was not in a hurry to get that table. I would walk around a bit and act like I was undecided. Then I would go to the specified table that I was instructed to look for. I never put the ball carrier on the pool table. That's how players do it. I placed my ball carrier on a cocktail table or counter near the table. Next I went to go find a stick, since I didn't bring mine. This was an extremely important step. When selecting a stick, I did not concern myself with how straight it was. All I needed to do was consider how much tip was left on the cue stick. I always tried to find a cue tip that emulates the one that was on my own stick. That way I could control the cue ball the same as when I practiced. After finding the best-tipped stick, I took it to my table, lay the stick flat on the table, and roll it around to verify its straightness. I could select a few sticks and take them back to my table, but I would have to roll them all. The reason I did this was simple: that's what nonplayers did. Most shooters can play with bent cue sticks all day. It is primarily because they have perfected their stroke. All these habits give everyone in the pool hall the perception that I have absolutely no idea what I was doing. It's kinda funny, huh?

Now that I have a table and I have a cue stick, I need to rack the balls. First, I may need to locate the actual rack. Some pool halls may give them to me when they issue the balls, but most of the time, the racks are by the table. They are located either under table or on the light over the table. I would take some time here looking for the rack unless it's real obvious. I can promise you I was always being watched. I kept up the act, because the fish were coming soon. I racked the balls a number of ways. I would put one ball in at a time . . . solid, stripe, solid, stripe . . . etc. I tried placing them in numerically. That takes way too long. Or I would take the ball carrier over to the table and just place all the balls in the rack randomly. I did not put the ball carrier on the table. I kept it in one hand while loading the balls in the rack. After racking the balls, I removed the rack and looked for a place to put it. I never put it back where I found it. I put the rack right on top of the ball carrier or wherever I placed it initially, maintaining the illusion, that I have never really played pool.

When I broke the rack up, I tried not to overdo it. Also, I did not use chalk until I miscued. There are two reasons for this. The first reason is obvious. When a shooter miscues, it makes an unmistakable sound that they just screwed up. The second reason was I needed to count how many shots I could get by chalking up one time before miscuing. I never chalked my stick after every shot. That was a dead giveaway that I was using English. I always made sure I miscued a couple of times, so I had a good feel for the tip, but I didn't get carried away. If I was shooting without using English, the chalk on the tip was not going to be a factor. Center ball shots or shots with "natural leave" are what I was going to use most of the time. My focus was more on ball speed and control. While shooting balls on my table, I would need to concentrate on the table roll, otherwise known as ball drift. The other thing was rail action. The worst thing in the world was playing on a table with dead rails. That means when I hit the rail, I would hear a loud knock. But that's not all. The rail would not respond to any English I had applied to the cue ball. For someone planning on controlling the table, this would be impossible, because the table would maintain control. That means I, as the shooter, would be at the mercy of the table. That's not going work out to well if I plan on going fishing on that table. I made sure when I was checking drift and rails, I didn't make too many shots. In fact, the only shots I wanted to make were the balls that were in my way while checking out the table action. I frequently hit some balls as hard as I could. This gave me a feel for the table's ball speed. I kept up this educational "ball banging" time for as long as an hour. Sometimes, like real fishing, I could get a bite before my first rack break was over. If I had never played on that table before, I'd never take the first fish that comes along. If someone approached me to play a game, I would just say, "I'm waiting for a friend to join me." The reason I would say that is to give myself some time to get comfortable with the table. When my task was complete, and my fictitious friend had not arrived, I would just sit down. I'd look at my watch or phone with a tired concerned or even bored look. Look up at the fishes every once in a while, and I would patiently watch what was about to happen. Within minutes, someone would want to play. If it was the first time playing that person, I would let them break. They may tell me to break since it was my table. So I would go ahead and break. If they broke, I would watch carefully if they are using any English and watch if they are running more than three to four balls. The average player can make three to four balls in a row. If they make more than that, it's very possible they know how to play too. This was a good thing and a bad thing for me. I may have caught the biggest fish in the place, and he is looking to play for lots of money. On the other hand, if I hustle him and win, no fish in the entire place is ever going near my table for the rest of the day. So it was a judgment call, based on lots of factors. Factors like what time is it? How much longer can I play for? How many other fish are here? How well and confident am I playing right now? When an opponent wanted to give me a game, it was rare that they would ask to play for money right out of the chute. They wanted some information, too—the same information that I was looking for. I have now, up to this point, been mistaken for a fish. They are unaware that I was, in fact, a fisherman.

When I played a new opponent, I was going to do a few things. I was taught that I was going to lose, and I'm going to lose by a lot. I didn't ever want to look like a threat. I was going to only make one or two balls in a row maximum. Never make more than that unless it was on accident. The reason was I needed to watch them take more shots than me. This allowed me to gain information on their strengths and the weakness. Is he consistent? Can he make bank shots? Does he know how to use English properly? Does he control the cue ball at all? If I'm shooting all the time, I cannot answer these questions.

Here comes what I call "The Script." It would normally come out around the second or third game. The player's lines started the same way every time. It would begin with me racking the balls. They always ask, "Do you want to make it interesting?" I would respond, "What do you mean?" They would continue, "Do you want to play for something?" I would ask, "What did you have in mind?" They would normally say, "How about five a game?" While this conversation is going, I would have walked over to the player to continue our pending verbal contract. They always seem to start at five dollars, mostly because they are weary of whom they're playing against. I would clarify, "Five dollars a game, huh?" As I said that, I would pull my money out of my pocket right in front of him. The twenty-dollar bill that I had placed on top would be very visible to him. My Tata showed me this trick. When I reached in my pocket and pulled something out, their eyes would always go directly to my hand to see what I had. I know, right? Try it with someone who has no reason to look down at what you are getting out of your pocket. My guess is that they'll still look. It's a play on human nature that I was prepared for. He wants to play for five dollars, and now he knows that I have at least twenty. So I agree to play for five dollars, and I continue to lose. I would continue to lose until "Act 2" of "The Script."

A normal opponent would begin "Act 2" after they win the second game. The reason is that they are now up two games to zero, and they have ten dollars of my money. They also know that I have twenty dollars. They have gained confidence and momentum. Again, the conversation starts the same way, while I'm racking for the next game. They would inquire, "Do you want to try double or nothing?" That would bump the bet for each game up to ten dollars. Now at this time, I would evaluate the player. Do I have a hook in him, or is he about to get away? If I feel he's about to get away, I would choose to win the next game, but I'd make it look like an accident. By doing this, it gave them the impression that I was lucky, and he walks away with zero dollars of my money. Now the ball is in his court. He may decide to continue to play or leave empty-handed. Again, it was rare that they would leave knowing that they had been kicking my butt, and now they have nothing to show for it. Most players' egos will not allow this to happen. So they would normally continue to play. If they did, I would win again. Again, I would barely win, and it would look like another accident. Now I'm up ten dollars. So begins "Act 3."

Back when he asked if I wanted to double the bet, I said to myself, "I have two choices." The second option was if I thought I got this fish hooked, I would lose again. Losing three games in a row would almost guarantee I would be playing the fish for a while. Now if I chose to lose the third game, I would be down twenty dollars. It's funny how this worked, but "Act 3" would still start at this point. The only difference was that in the first scenario, I'm up ten dollars, and in the second scenario, I'm down twenty dollars. So this time, depending on whoever was breaking the next game's rack, would start the dialog. If I had the break and was up ten dollars, I would say, "Double or nothing?" Or if I was racking, and they, being up twenty dollars, they would ask, "Double or nothing?" Either way this goes, we were now playing for twenty dollars a game. This was the average dollar amount most hustlers shoot for. At this point, I had a fish on the line. I would normally continue to win until he quit or owed me so much he couldn't afford to play.

If I executed this correctly, that player whom I got on the hook will want to try to get his money back by playing me over and over again. The reason that happens was their own ego blinds them, and their own pride prevents them from giving up. When this happens, I had gone from having "a fish" to "a cash cow." All this player knew was that he beat me in the beginning, and I'm just the luckiest pool player alive.

Of course, I had played this hustle to a much higher level—to the tune of one-thousand-dollar sets. But like I said before, most players hover around twenty to fifty dollars. Remember, I didn't want to scare all the fish away. I was extremely cautious and very careful when I took people's money like this. It could have had some painful and damaging outcomes. I can say I was very lucky that no one ever got physical with me. If they ever had come to the conclusion that I had hustled them, I would have to perform "Act 4."

"Act 4" would be me trying to escape the pool hall with my life and my limbs. I figured if that happened regularly, I would really have to work on my patience when shooting or my acting. If they, for one second, noticed I was a fisherman, and I sensed this inclination, I would start yawning and leave before they could make a scene. Remember, I was the star of the show, not them. The audience always paid to see the performance. The performer walked away with the money. Sometimes I would even run.

When I've described these steps to other players, they just look at me with an amazed stare. Then they confess that this had happened to them before. I always tell them that if they weren't aware of these steps, it's easy to get hustled. I have never seen these steps written in any book or any Billiards instruction manual. Apparently, it's an art that has been passed down from one hustler to another hustler. In this case, my grandfather passed all his knowledge to me. I am explaining the steps so that you know what to look for in a hustle. One of the worst feelings in the world is knowing that you were just hustled.

Chapter 7

The Navy

Can you believe that I actually started hustling people around ages twelve or thirteen? I would get in money games a couple of times a week. I would get a taker either at the bowling alley, arcade, or pool hall. We never really played for massive amounts of money. Most games were from a dollar up to maybe twenty dollars. It really depended on whether it was a kid or an adult that I found to play. I played more pool between the ages thirteen to fifteen mainly to stay cool. It was something to do inside and stay out of the sun. When I turned sixteen, I had enough money to buy a car. Once I began driving, I needed the money more for gas, insurance, and upkeep of the car. Although I still played, I didn't have time to play as much.

As a junior in high school, I was busier with more school activities, like varsity band and varsity golf. I still had my paper route after school too. So playing pool was not a priority, but I got into a few games here and there. My best friend, Allan, would come over and play to pass the time. We would talk about what we were going to do after high school. I had entered the Navy's Delayed Entry Program at the age of seventeen. This basically meant that I was enlisted in the Navy and was serving one year of inactive duty while finishing high school. I wasn't exactly crazy about school in general. I did what I had to do to get good enough grades to pass and graduate. I graduated with a 3.8 GPA, after having a really difficult junior year. My GPA during my first junior semester had dropped down to a 1.9. My father was not happy about this at all. Let me just say, without going into detail, he knew how to keep me motivated and get me back on track. Looking back on that time, I have since realized that all I was concerned about was my car, my friends, music, and, of course, girls. Yes, mostly in this order. Yup, I was typical for a teenage boy.

I had my paper route for over six years before I graduated. Two weeks after graduation, I was in a place called MEPS (Military Entrance Processing Station) located in San Diego, California. This was like a foreign country all in itself. I never really had been away from home before. I was not worried or scared or anything. It felt weird just being out on my own for the first time. I was still being told where to go and what to do, just by other people. It felt like I was under new management. In a sense, that would prove to be true. I was in Navy boot camp from July to August of '87 and was stationed at Naval Training Center San Diego for Basic Electricity and Electronics (BEE) School and Interior Communications "A" School. I remember getting up at six in the morning daily for duty station muster and daily cleanup assignments. The enlistees would then go to breakfast and be in class by 0800 hours. Classes would end around 1500, or even 1530. This was a perfect time to do laundry and eat dinner. After that, if I was not on duty, I could do pretty much whatever I wanted. Lots of sailors would go out to the movies, or they would go to the beach. Most of my classmates were still under twenty-one years of age, so they could not drink off base. However, they could drink on-base with their military identification card. It was typical that some of the guys would end up spending all their money before the next payday. Since most of us were between the E1 and E3 pay grades, we didn't make much money. If my memory serves me right, I believe I was making about $340 every two weeks.

On pay day, at the time, the Navy would pay everyone in cash. A pay truck would pull up literally in front of our barracks, and we would line up for our pay disbursement. This pay distribution process intrigued me. Everyone had cash in his hands, and everyone else knew it. It made for another opportunity for me. I had learned some of the guys never had money before or had a job that earned them a paycheck. Some of these guys were the same guys who did not know how to manage their paycheck for two weeks. They would seem to run out of money before the next payday constantly, mostly because they would drink too much. It was amazing to me how many guys could not control their spending habits, especially when it came to alcohol. Some of these guys found out that I didn't drink and that I always had money on hand. So I would have been considered a loan shark on base. They would come up to me and ask if I could loan them money. Sometimes, it was one or two days before payday, but they couldn't wait, especially if it was a weekend. I would loan them whatever amount we had agreed on with an interest agreement attached. An example would be twenty dollars for thirty dollars. The best part about it was I knew when they would have the cash to pay me back. So after getting paid, I would stand by, waiting for everyone to receive their cash at the pay truck, collect their debt, and then scratch their name off my little green memo book. I would make so much money on the interest; it was like having another paycheck. Needless to say, I was a popular guy before every payday, but not on payday.

Like I said before, after class, I could do anything I wanted. So with the extra money, I would find myself at the base bowling alley or recreation room. They had around ten nine-foot pool tables. I would play an average of eight hours a night. The best part about it was every two weeks there were new fish to hustle. Some players would show up every week trying to get back what they lost, but most would be new players who thought they could play. I did this the entire time I was in school, from August of '87 to about May of '88. During this time, I had fine-tuned my shooting. My safety shots and patience had become so good that everyone I played knew they could beat me. All you had to do was ask them. Still, they never walked away with any money. It's amazing how their egos kept them blind to that fact.

After communication school, I was ordered to report to my first ship at Naval Base 32nd Street, San Diego. I was stationed there for six months before that ship was decommissioned. Then I was reassigned to my second ship that was a couple of piers over. While stationed onboard a ship, if I wasn't underway, I would still be hustling players in my free time. When underway, I would play cards and Dominos to keep my competitive instincts alive. Now, about this time in my life, I was nineteen years old and an E4 in the Navy. I was carrying anywhere from five hundred dollars to two thousand dollars in cash just to hustle pool. I was playing over forty hours of pool a week easily, unless I was out to sea. I was making more money playing pool than as a full-time United States sailor. I did the math. It turns out I played over ten thousand hours from 1987 to 1991.

By doing what I was doing, I thought my dad would be proud of me. Although he was proud that I was serving in our United States Navy, he was extremely disappointed in me after I bragged of how much money I was making playing pool. He came up to me, put his finger in my chest, and said, "Don't ever tell me how much money you stole from someone." He continued, "Why don't you play in real pool tournaments? Then we'll see just how good you really are." My immaturity, ego, and pride would not allow me to understand what my father was trying to express to me at the time. He was warning me about how my character and moral values were being deceived by the enemy. He stated that if I continued my ways of lying and cheating people out of their money, I would probably be injured permanently or dead. Unfortunately, all I did was ignore his heartfelt warning. He left me alone, and I didn't bring it up in any conversations again. Deep down in my spirit, I knew he was speaking the truth, and he was trying to help me grow as an individual.

My dad allowed my character to grow, and for the next few years, I played in two or three tournaments every week when I wasn't underway. I was still hustling, though. I just couldn't turn off that switch. After all, I had been hustling for almost ten years. I never shared any of this with my Tata, but I'm sure my dad did. I never thought of hustling as a character flaw, but as an adult, now I understand what my father was speaking to me about. All I had become was an educated thief or con man. My dad knew and understood what I had become. This justified why he felt sadness toward my so-called success.

Chapter 8

The Seed

During most of my naval career, I was dating my wife. Kristy was going to college and was in class or working most of the time. On a rare occasion, she would come watch me play pool. Most of the time, she would attend a tournament that I was competing in. Every once in a while, I would get someone who wanted to play for money. She would see how my focus and attitude would change during a match. I recall her stating that "I'm in another world" or "I don't hear anything that is happening around me." She claimed that she would talk to me, and I would never respond as if I never heard a word she said. I was so locked in to what I was doing that I wasn't me anymore. This happened a few times, and it seemed to bother her. To be completely honest, it did bother me. It felt like I had stepped outside of myself, and the person actually playing wasn't even me. It started to feel like I was a machine with no emotions.

I can remember a couple of years after my dad had planted the seed in my mind about changing my deceiving ways. I had been playing just as much pool as I ever had. Kristy and I probably had just gone to dinner or something. We ended up back at the Navy base so I could play pool. There was a guy there who wanted to play. Everything was the same as always. We played a few games, and after an hour or two, I was up almost $250. There was something that was different, though; the guy I was playing had his wife and young child with him. He was a little older than I was. He could not have been any older than twenty-three. While we were playing, my eyes would catch his wife looking more and more disappointed and concerned about the money. I could see how she would give him a look of disrespect and anger. Strangely, I didn't seem as focused as I normally was. Looking back at that game, I believe God had given me a glimpse of things to come. I noticed their young child looked hungry, and Momma looked tired. At that moment, I realized what my father was talking about. The young father who was trying to make more money playing pool was just as sick as I was. The only difference was he had a wife and kid, and I didn't. I walked away from the game, saying to myself, "By the grace of God, there go I." I was twenty-one years old, and the seed of character that my dad had planted in my mind two years earlier had not only taken root but had sprouted into an oak tree. I would love to tell you that I gave all the money back to that family, but I didn't. I was so confused and beside myself. The conflict that was happening within me was so overwhelming that all I remember is sobbing while leaving the table. This was the last time I ever hustled anyone for money.

I refer to gambling and hustling as a sickness to many people I have talked to over the years. Some people understand, and some just look at me with a confused stare. I try to explain to them, like any other "high" you would get from alcohol or drugs: if you do it too much, it can be an addictive and destructive path for your life. I'm so fortunate that I recognized that I had an issue. Also, people in my life allowed me to figure out my priorities. It took some time, but I can say I feel that I am a better person for overcoming this stronghold on my life. God's grace is good.

I continued to play in tournaments all over San Diego and on base. I quit hiding my ability to play. I would find myself playing some of the best players in Southern California. I would also play in tournaments in Long Beach, Anaheim, and Irvine. Although I met some fine shooters and even played a few games of 9-Ball with Jeanette "The Black Widow" Lee, tournament play had become routine. I would place first, second, or third every week in almost every tournament. Playing pool was never boring. Some players would say, "The game is no fun unless you're playing for something." I always like when they'd say," I bet you couldn't even play if there was money involved." They would say this because when I would play for fun,

I could shoot relaxed. When I shoot relaxed, I didn't miss much. It would make my spirit laugh inside.

Meeting new people and making new friends was always nice too. I was actually 86ed from some tournaments because when I showed up, everyone else would leave. That means that I was banned from coming to their tournament. I talked to the owners and tournament directors about this issue, and I agreed to stay away so their businesses wouldn't lose money. I never wanted to be the cause of someone losing money again. When playing in a tournament, I did not have to act like I didn't know how to play to win. The games went a lot faster than when I was trying to hustle someone. After playing years in tournaments, I would have players ask me for shot advice and shooting strategies. Helping someone raise their level of play is an awesome feeling. Now I know how my Tata felt every time I executed a shot that he had showed me.

I still love shooting a great game of pool. Sometimes friends whom I have been playing with for years will call me to see if I want to shoot some. I can't help wanting to teach them everything I know. Some want the knowledge, and some don't. I don't mind either way. I'm just glad they call. I am so grateful that my dad planted that seed, or else I may not have any friends who play pool. I could have been dead in an alley somewhere. I may have never made it to the church altar to marry my wonderful bride. I could still be an unsaved soul and lost forever in the lies of the enemy. Thank you, Jesus, for giving me eyes to see and ears to hear.

Chapter 9

The Answer

All of this information, I am embarrassed to say, is true. I'm not proud of the money I hustled from all the naïve players over that early decade of my life. However, if God hadn't allowed me to go through the deception of what I thought success was or, better said, what Satan had told me success was, I wouldn't have the knowledge to educate my own children on what God's idea of prosperity really is. Many people have congratulated me for winning pool tournaments. I can promise you, the wins were not mine to take credit for. All that I am, and all that I'm becoming is by the grace of God.

I was introduced to many influential people who knew what true success was. Fortunately for me, I became friends with many of them. One of them told me, "If you lose some money, you've lost nothing. If you lose a friend, you've lost something. If you've lost your word, you've lost everything." My honest word had been lost for quite some time. I didn't know how to regain my wounded character. They would begin to show Kristy and me what God's will was for our lives. They have been a huge blessing to both of us. I personally have gained an understanding of how I should be as a man, a husband, and a father. I have never been perfect, and I have come to realize that I will never be. Now I look to gain love and respect from my wife and children by becoming what God wants. I'm a never-ending work in progress.

There are specific things that I am grateful for—things that I never would have thought I would ever enjoy in my lifetime. Most guys talk about a fast sports car, traveling the world, or going to a huge sporting event. Nope, I'm a much simpler person than that. I would aspire to have my own nine-foot regulation pool table at home so I could teach my kids and anyone else how to play the wonderful game of Pocket Billiards. This dream had become a reality for me this last year. My generous mother-in-law had decided to downsize her home. She didn't have room in her new house to accommodate the pool table that she had purchased for the game room for the entire family in the previous home. Kristy had gone to help her mother move from one house to the other, and her mom asked if we would take the pool table. When Kristy returned home, she had told me what her mom had offered us. My wife knew my heart, and she knew I would accept this precious gift.

I spent the next five months remodeling and preparing our home for the new addition. As if I was expecting another child. I wanted to be completed with the remodel and have the table up in time for Father's Day. I was determined; and with persistence, hard work, and help from my Uncle Al and son Kacey, we accomplished the task by Memorial Day. I have asked God, "What is prosperity? What does it look like?" My full heart is just a glimpse of what true prosperity is. The Lord has bigger plans for me. I can feel it. I have allowed his will for my life instead of my will. I don't know what God has in store for me and my family, but I know more trials will be coming. I've learned the more challenges I am faced with the more blessings I will obtain.

I look back on those early adult years and wonder what would have happened had I continued living for the hustle, when, in fact, I was truly gambling. I could keep the false success that Satan was handing me or repent and have God open my eyes to what true prosperity actually is. I realized at the age of twenty-one that I was actually the one being hustled. The stakes were much higher than I had agreed on. I was never willing to gamble with my salvation. My soul was not negotiable. Satan had been playing me for thirteen years. He would be patient in the playing of his own game. He baited me with money at a young age. He gave me success by lying and deceiving. He allowed me to be addicted so I had a false sense of accomplishment. He would boost my ego and pride so I would think highly of myself. I was destined to lose. This was the evil one's plan all along. How crazy is this? It looks exactly like what I spoke about in chapter 6, right?

I will soon be fifty years old and have been married for almost twenty-five years to the most beautiful woman I have ever had the privilege of knowing. I have five wonderful kids whom I completely adore. In time, I hope they'll know and understand this story of my salvation so they can learn from it. My prayer is that they know that God is all knowing and all loving. He will provide their needs and bless them in his time.

I have dreamt of writing this book not for me, but to give credit to my father and grandfather. They both have inspired me in different ways. Both had their shortcomings, challenges, and demons to overcome. Also, for my children and future grandchildren to know that they're a blessing to everyone they come in contact with. As my dad would say, "You're a feather in my cap." This was how he expressed how proud he was of me.

So, Zachary, to answer your question . . . Yeah, I have played in a pool tournament before. Not only am I still playing, but also it's still my shot.

Rack 'em!

Romans 8:28: "And we know that all things work together for good to them that love God, to them who are called according to his purpose."

About the Author

Marcos Carvajal was born and raised in Yuma, Arizona. He graduated as a Yuma Criminal from Yuma High School in 1987, became
president of the Yuma High Marching Band, and was a four-year
Letterman on the Varsity Golf Team. He enlisted in the United States
Navy after high school and became an interior communications electrician for eight and a half years. He got married in 1994 and pro-
ceeded to have five wonderful children. He accepted Jesus Christ
as his personal Savior at 12:30 p.m. on a Sunday, April 30, 1995.
He was baptized with his bride at Skyline Wesleyan Church in La
Mesa, California which was previously pastored by Orval Butcher,
John C. Maxwell and currently pastored by Dr. James L. Garlow.
He has attended Skyline Church since 1994 and is currently a full-
time low-voltage communications electrician and PBX programmer
in San Diego, California.

9 781643 494364